Luscious Love Lines
A Collection of Romantic and Intimate Poetry...

Thomas Ricardo Baker

ISBN:
9798831909098

DEDICATION

This collection is dedicated to all of the lovers of romantic, intimate poetry, cool jazz music, quiet nights with your special someone, and aficionados of good food, fine wine, rich coffee, and treasured friendships. NEVER stop dreaming and working towards everything in your power to make your dreams reality. May everything that you do in your life be luscious, filled with lots of love and may the words you speak, the actions that you do, and the love you give touch the hearts, minds, and souls of everyone in your lives.

VERY SPECIAL DEDICATIONS

To Rhyme N' Chatt, a wonderful group of poets and poetesses from hometown of Chattanooga, Tennessee, U.S.A.: Thank you for creating a platform for lyrical artistry and poetic excellence to be expressed in the Scenic City

To Marsha Mills, Brainerd High School Class of '86:
Thank you for always being encouraging and creative, for you are one of the greatest poetesses that I've ever known...:"Yo' Love"(Ode to Miles Davis), is still one of my favorite pieces ever...my goal is to write and perform my poetry as hot and sizzling as you do

To the Orchard Knob Middle School Poetry Slam Society (2000-2005):
Thank you for being one of most dynamic groups of writers and performers ever as well as being a group that was sooooo much fun to work with...

To the Lindley Middle School Poetry Slam Society(2005-2013):
Thank you for being an amazing group of students, writers and performers of poetry and prose

To the Friday night "Sip n' Flow" crew from Lillian's Coffeehouse in Mableton, Georgia, U.S.A.(2006-2008):
Lorna Reddicks!!! Thank you for allowing me to host and perform in such a wonderful venue. We had such great times!!! You allowed "Da Cappuccino Brotha" to do his thing!!! Also, Arlene "Sista Queen" Scott and my brother, Kevin Stafford...I love you guys forever and ever!!!

My "Sistas" Support Group:
Andronica Byrd, Deidre Sims, Bonnie Lockhart, Melinda Ward...Thank you for ALWAYS having my back, supporting me in my spiritual AND career endeavors. Your love for me has helped me through the most difficult of times...may Jehovah God continue to bless you.

The residents of Pfeiffer-Stagmaier dorm at University of Tennessee at Chattanooga, 89-90:
I love you all! SOOOO many cherished memories from and of all of you. The year that I spent with you changed my life forever...

My family, The Wilsons and The Bakers:
Fam! Thank you for ALWAYS having my back and supporting me in my life! I hope and pray that I am making you proud...

Moma:
I could've NEVER done this without you!!! I love you
forever…to the moon and back…

CONTENTS

ACKNOWLEDGMENTS

Dr. Chloe Garth-Elkins:
Meeting you at the Howard School of Academics and Technology changed my life FOREVER!!! Not only did you send letters to Oprah in my behalf concerning the original manuscript of Luscious Love Lines, but you supported me in ascension as a novelist and aspiring songwriter as well. Also, you encouraged me to become an English Teacher, making sure that I (and my future students…)had all of the tools needed to have success. Due to this beautiful career, I've had the honor of traveling the world, from Sao Paulo to Dubai, teaching talented and thoughtful youth, lovers of the English language. I owe it all to you!!!

Darrick Hardwick:
You are the best friend and brother one could ever have. I thank you for your years of love, support, friendship, not to mention your immense graphic design skills, and out of this world creativity. May Jehovah continue to bless you and Monica.

Eric Latimore, Sr., aka "Sonny Snowflake":
You are my brother FOREVER! My life changed when you arrived at the Lithia Springs Congregation back in 2014. Who knew what Jehovah would have in store for us? Thank you for ALWAYS supporting and encouraging me in my spiritual, career, and artistic endeavors. May Jehovah continue to bless you and Shon.

To the "Ocean's 5 family and crew:
Our original crew of five is now a group of 13, 14, 15… lol! You brothers have always supported my hopes and dreams, not only as a man, but as a SPIRITUAL man. Thank you for everything! When I get back to the "A", PLEASE have that Crown Royal Peach waiting on me!!! Lolol!!!

A Luscious Love Line

I got into my poetic frame of mind
I unleashed fragrant vanilla candlelight
As my dreams and fears for a spiritual love
This candle would ignite
Due to my evening's mood and this candle's
evocative scent
The time would be perfect for some luscious love
lines to invent
So I reminisced on good times and sweet love
Trials lovers go through and share
How deeply two become one
Giving every ounce of themselves
How deeply for that special love I would care

Looking outside, a star dances
As the moon enhances
The many intimate emotions
that make special romances
Soon clouds separate
During my private state
I think and ponder
On that true love that I know I deserve
And on that, I'll patiently wait

Yet, inside very soul,
my own quiet storm is erupting
But not interrupting
My thought processing
Because despite all of the struggles,
the hurt and pain
I realize that true love is a blessing
So I write, I pen, I compose
I suppose, something exquisite and lush
That causes a rush to my pulsating heart,
As soon during this midnight stillness
My thoughts will come to a hush
Allowing me to come up with something
Eternally divine
Crafted from the loins of my soul,
The depths of my heart,
That will cause tears to well up in her eyes,
And a tingle to run up and down her spine
As I blow out the candle, the wick still fragrant,
I know she's on cloud nine,
For I just tapped into her innermost thoughts
With a luscious love line

Rose Petals

Rose Petals
Rose petals
All over you
Rose petals
Rose petals
A most special thing to do
In my secret garden
I fantasize
I'm moved deeply
By the love in your eyes
Rose petals falling
Gently from my fingertips
Strawberry kisses
All over my body
From your luscious lips
The time for love is now
At this moment I must exude
Something sensual and seductive
Creating the perfect mood
All over your body
Rose petals soothing you
Emotional tranquility
Sweetness only I would provide for you

Rose Petals
Rose petals
All over you
Rose petals
Rose petals
A most special thing to do

One look at you
I perceive the things
Your body will say
As I handsomely
Sprinkle petals all over
Your body as we lay
You're enamored with the love I give
The oil on your body,
the kisses upon your skin
It's as if each petal that I
bestow upon you touches your soul
bringing forth the love
you hold deeply within
I massage deeper…deeper…
From your elegant shoulders
to the small of your back
I can't believe we're living in the moment…
tiny candle-lit flames gently willowing
amidst a palette of midnight and black

I only pray that I could be one of the petals
Drifting upon your skin so rich,
so chocolate, so espresso, so ebony,
With every petal that falls upon your skin
I'm so aroused…tell me…
What is it that you do to me?

Rose Petals
Rose petals
All over you
Rose petals
Rose petals
A most special thing to do

This moment that we share together
It's so surreal, so heavenly
May we share love like this again?
I'd be honored
I mean that quite supremely
From this day until eternity

Nothing in this world would
Mean as much to me
As the ecstasy and pleasure
on your face I see
every time I sprinkle
rose petals all over
your body

Delectable

Delectable…
Like the succulent chocolate given to you by a
special, intimate lover
Delectable…
Like the sweetest of sweet talk uttered by your
"significant lover",
So sexy undercover
Delectable…
Like soft, misty raindrops that descend effortlessly
From the midsummer sky meekly upon your skin
Delectable…
Like a long-awaited, never-ending French kiss…
When does it end, where does it begin?
Delectable…
Like a woman in sensual, open-toed shoes
With well-pedicured, sexy, kissable toes…
How tasty you are…only God knows
Delectable…delectable…delectable

Red is the color...

Red is the color...
Of that fragrant rose, the one that I choose,
Smelling oh, so sweet, just beneath your nose
Red is the color...
That makes my heart beat faster,
makes my chest pulsate
The sight of it blows my mind
at a quick and accentuated rate
Red is the color...
Of strawberry candlelight that gently
burns through the night,
When it's on like this,
You must confer that I will do you right
Red is the color...
When you blush and smile from the
winsome words I speak,
It's all about you, so fresh and unique,
Red is the color...
Of a most expensive wine
The chardonnay we sip every time we dine,
Red is the color...
Of a mini-skirt, a tantalizing dress
accented with a pocketbook, a silk blouse,

Worn with style and finesse;
Red is the color…
Of my satin lingerie that I like to see you in,
you're wearing it, lovin' me again and again,
What a pleasant reprise;
Girl, you make my heart rejoice, bringing
Ecstasy to my body and pleasure to my eyes;
Red is the color…
Of candied apples, autumn leaves falling from the
trees,
The shiny coat of polish on those sexy, kissable toes,
Causing me to think ahead of us chillin' at those
jazz shows,
Listening to those saxy beats and grooves,
While poets and poetesses deliver their lyrical flows
Summer concerts in the park,
Picnic baskets, grapes, chicken and cheese,
I'll provide the flame, you'll provide the spark;
As your sweetness will bring me to my knees

Red is the color…
Of the lip gloss on those succulent lips…
Can I kiss them, taste them as I hold
that waist and caress those hips?
Red is the color…

That I love to see you wear on our first date,
Vibrant, seductive, first-class, first-rate,
Causing me to ponder on boxes of heart-shaped
chocolates
Scented carnations, tiny cherries in
Shirley Temples;
As I watch you sip, I'm turned on by
the sight of your deep dimples
Unlike any other...
Red is the color...

Strawberry Candlelight

Today at work all I did was daydream
I saw your eyes sparkle, I saw them gleam
I saw you holding me, caressing me,
And as continued to dream about you
kissing me and loving me, I thought for a
*split second, "**This** is how good a love should be…"*
So I began to make our evening's plans,
They would involve lots of intimacy,
A great deal of romance,
a scenario in which we could talk,
hold hands and slow dance;
I've thought about this time,
at least once or twice,
Many have had suggestions,
Others, wisdom and advice;
True, she loves roses,
Velvet red, lavender, yellow,
They always smell nice;
But tonight, only flowers won't suffice,
We'll have strawberry candlelight, dinner,
Some wine over ice…
Candid conversation…just right to entice

So you name the place and
I'll set the site
Sweet love
Strawberry candlelight
I'll set the mood for a most precious night
Just you
Strawberry Candlelight
Soft and sweet, discreetly scented
Your love
Strawberry Candlelight
Sharing love only we've invented
Good love
Strawberry Candlelight

We need to share
some time all alone
No outside distractions, no family,
no work, no cell phone
Baby, on this, I insist
For a sexy mood is in our midst,
This moment I can't resist
Put on the jazz, soft and low
Or a sensuous love song with that
Seductive vocal flow

I know that every lady loves chocolate
And sweet perfume
They are expressions of love,
Romantic, I presume
But tonight I want to provide you
With something unique, so gratifying,
A tantalizing delight,
A candle exuding that strawberry scent,
Alone with you as I wrap that body tight

So you name the place and
I'll set the site
Sweet love
Strawberry candlelight
I'll set the mood for a most precious night
Just you
Strawberry Candlelight
Soft and sweet, discreetly scented
Your love
Strawberry Candlelight
Sharing love only we've invented
Good love
Strawberry Candlelight

Vibacious

I felt it when she walked by,
It registered when she spoke to me
like a soft, gentle tremor moving through me
Her eyes captivated me with their
gentle sensitivity;
Longing to notice if what she felt was the same as I,
The vibe beckoned me, too
About this I could not lie;
It was real through and through;
She was sexy, but not salacious,
Inviting, but not flirtacious;
Cool, alluring, energetic…yes vibacious
You see, this lady had a certain energy,
Delicate electricity, she had, if I could create
A new word…vi-ba-ci-ty;
Yes, with style and graciousness,
girlfriend touched me;
Wearing wide-legged pants,
Fashionable, urbane,
Looking so delicious, driving me insane,
With that one-inch cuff,
She's too much, yet not enough
Wearing shoes so shiny that one can tell

That these pumps never missed a weekly buff
Her shoes were made of a most exquisite leather;
Lady is gorgeous, yes she is together;
Yeah, she's luscious, very aware of Victoria's Secret
But there's no loving before marriage, her goodies,
Her sweet love-she'll keep it,
To herself, not mystified by
an immature man's game
Or materialistic wealth;
She's about giving to others, displaying
unselfishness,
Being kind to others, while maintaining emotional
stability,
Being noticed, yet remaining stealth;
So as I watched her prance into my favorite coffee
shop;
Somewhere between old-school cool
and new world exotica;
Classic, mellow jazz and bumpin' hip-hop,
I had to think about it once more as I came to a
stop:
She was sexy, but not salacious,
Inviting, but not flirtacious;
Cool, alluring, energetic...yes vibacious

Where Did You Get Those Shoes?

*Excuse me for asking, but where did you get those
shoes?*
Oh, my, they're so nice, they look so good on you
I love the way your foot fits inside your shoe
*Cappuccino-colored, even espresso, that shoe looks
so good on you*

*Excuse me for asking, but where did you get those
shoes?*
Oh, my, they're so nice, they look so good on you
*When you walk into the room nonchalant, yet
stylin',*
*The stiletto heels, so very tall, caught my eye, so
elegant,*
Are they Italian?
You dress with so much flavor,
Classy, conservative,
The type of flair that any man would want to savor
The way you look in that business suit,
Shapely, a figure that will not quit
Professionalism, feminine, strong and delicate
*I'm impressed with the fashion and clothes you
choose,*

Please, tell me where did you get those shoes?
Excuse, me for asking, but where did you get those shoes?
Oh, my, they're so nice they look so good on you
I want to know to get a pair for my wife
To increase the romance, spice up my love life
My mate loves it when I show her honor and thoughtfulness
Believe me when I say that it's a love that way God could bless
You see there's something sexy about a man
Carrying a beautiful gift-wrapped package,
So I've heard…better than sweet kisses or kind words,
So for the sake of love, romance and happiness,
Don't lead me on, or hold back any clues,
Just tell me…please…where did you get those shoes?

Please...Lie With Me, My Wife

Please...Lie With Me, My Wife
And let me give you love
To satisfy you for your entire life
Entice me with your silhouette
Remember?
The one that blew my mind
the first time we met?
Though I must admit
Your beauty floors me
Yes...you baby, so gently in
The midst of candles softly lit

Please...Lie With Me, My Wife
And allow me to know
Your dreams through love expression,
For now we are man and wife,
Never will there be a wrong move
or a bad impression
I'm always so into you: what you desire,
What you need,
Your love is so, so good to me
That it moves me to take heed

Please…Lie With Me, My Wife
I ask that if you even though
I really don't have to
Praise, honor and respect
Are accorded to you
By how I speak, express
and make love to you
So let me render to you
Your romantic and intimate due

I Want To Make Love To Your Mind

The art of romance is ever-changing
All of these ups and downs and re-arranging
All of those lustful propositions
But I listen to my mind and feel my intuitions
What's happened to being a gentleman
Courteous and kind?
I need a love, real and true, so divine
So let me respect you and make love to your mind
I want to make love to your mind
I want to stimulate your intellect
I want to make love to your mind
Respect and cherish your body
All of your moral standards I will respect
I want to make love to your mind
Thrill you with conversation
I want to make love to your mind
Soon give sweet love without reservation
Allow me to treat you sweet,
We'll have a little fun, just talk awhile
I know the meaning of discreet
So let me melt your heart with
My manners and style
Too often we talk about only sex

Its infatuated glory
But love made outside the bedroom
Tells the real story
True lovers know that
Trust breeds intimacy
For when you love one another's minds,
The rest comes easily

I want to make love to your mind
Walk hand-in-hand on a midnight stroll
I want to make love to your mind
Embracing your heart and soul
I want to make love to your mind
Showing you honesty and sincerity
I want to make love to your mind
For that's sweet a love and romance should be

I Can't Wait

I can't wait
To partake…
Of kisses that will
Make a man quake…
Yes, girl…I know what's at stake…
Ecstasy so intense that after sharing
Such a deep love
Our bodies as one would shiver and shake
Imagine…how sweet and sensual a love
We would make
Follow my lead…let's play a romantic game
Of give and take
Let me give you hugs,
Shower your body with kisses
May each one gently touch your heart
Satisfying every single one of your wishes
Allow me to take you to a place
Where you'll be pleased
Pleased with all of the things that
I'll do to you
Too good to believe?
Concerning this chocolate sensuality
That I'll put on you?

Yes, baby…yes, baby…it is so, so true
This place where I'll take you
Is considered my special love
Mu God-given treasure,
The depth, width, extent of my love for you
No one could possibly measure
Stay here with me, in this place
So that we can share this
abundance of pleasure
I can see the look of love in your eyes
Cute, tiny beads of perspiration
glistening all over
your body as you imagine just how sumptuously
good this love would taste
So don't hesitate…
You name the place; I'll set the time and date
No matter where it is,
I'll be there…
Because girl, I can't wait

I Know How To Love You

I know how to love you
The way that you need to be loved
A different time, another place
The same flavor, a most exquisite taste
Many men come and go
They may try to get with you and enhance your
flow
But little do they know
I know just what to do
To make you happy, to satisfy your desire
I say it simply, "I know how to love you"

I know how to love you
You need a man that's God-fearing
Adhering to the teachings of truth,
Mature, sensitive, past the bloom of youth
He needs to be a strong, spiritual head,
Keeping you upbuilt and well-fed,
Christ-like, putting God first,
Knowing the right thing to say, the kind word
To quench your spiritual and emotional thirst

I know how to love you
You need a man
that can cook you dinner
from time to time
You would treasure my wealth
As your personal chef
I love creating tasty, sumptuous dishes
That are healing to the soul, good for your health

I know how to love you
I'd give you candlelight many a night
I'd give you a true love, candid conversation
Something much, much deeper than mere infatuation
We would talk deep into the night and early morning,
Satisfying your need for intimacy and attention,
The things for which your heart are yearning…
All while the seductive looks from my cappuccino-brown eyes
Give you ample warning…it's time for the debt to be paid,
Due rendered and love to be made

I know how to love you
I'd appreciate your body
All of its richness and mocha latte thickness
The sensual curvaceousness
I'd always be excited
By your sexy ways,
All of your lusciousness;
Chocolate covered strawberries…
I'd feed them to you
As I caress your body
Ecstasy…I'd take you there

My lips would kiss every pore
of your flesh,
From your neck to your breasts,
To your feet…to that plush derriere
Every touch I give you
Will show you how much I care

I know how to love you
I'll make your body shake and quake
In ecstasy when you lie next to me
Although I'd be so strong when I come inside,

I'd love you with gentleness and care,
I'd love you tenderly and sweetly

I know how to love you
I listen to you and understand what you need;
From spiritual to emotional
From romantic to physical
I'd love you unconditionally, whole-heartedly,
I'd be forever devotional
In everything that I would do
I would show you that
I know how to love you

Ethiopian Queen on the Seashore

In the late afternoon, a few hours before sundown
on the Persian Gulf
An Ethiopian queen takes in the moment on the
seashore
Her hair dances and flows amidst the warm
summer breezes with the tides rushing to the shore
from the sea...
Longing...desiring...wishing to caress her body in
natural, luxuriant waves of turquoise blue
that gently splash sensuality all over her supple,
rich chocolate skin that has been kissed and
gingered
by the delicate rays of the African sun for a lifetime
It's immaculately beautiful and soul soothing to
watch her enjoy herself in the peaceful tranquility
and serenity of the sea...
As she walks on the shore,
the sand softly and seductively tickles and
tantalizes her toes
Her cinnamon brown eyes sparkle and glisten
as she makes footprints in the golden sand,
Smiling in amazement as if she can't believe the
sheer beauty of what she is experiencing

As all of this is unfolding before me, I continue to
watch her and I can't help but wonder in sheer
amazement
For she looks so happy,
with her smile radiating such unbridled joy

The way that she moves with such grace and
freeness expresses the happiness that she possesses
deep within her
And at that very moment it occurs to me…
In this moment at sea, in this emotional break from
the everyday perils of life that this strikingly
gorgeous figment of chaste femininity is taking for
HERSELF,
innately bringing out all the natural beauty and
elegance of this Ethiopian queen..
And she is unselfishly sharing her emotions with
me,
Allowing me to feel all of the sweetness, love, joy
and selflessness that she is emanating from the
depths of her heart
Every smile, every bit of laughter, every kiss that
she blows shows love
I love you too, my Ethiopian Queen on the Seashore

Wedding Dress

*Every man adores and appreciates a woman that
looks good and smells good;
Who takes care in her physical beauty, yet works
diligently to bathe and enrich herself in deep
spirituality
I love your style and dress,
How you look in your attire
Classy and fashionable
Warm and loveable
So unbelievable
Absolutely incredible
Your gracefulness puts me in
A state of bliss
While little boys that are supposed to be men
Only care about how you effortlessly fill out your
jeans
The vision of you in radiant white and sparkling
lace
Makes me come undone at the seams;
I realize that most men want to see you attired*

skimpily or in nothing at all

That shows that they are only fleshly;

For if that's ALL I thought of you,

You would think less of me,

And that's not the gentleman that I strive to be;

That would make me quite immature

As I want to keep my opinion of you

beautifully candid, honest, and pure;

You could wear a nice pair slacks,

Elegant, flowing from just above the waist,

Paired with a silk blouse, it would be stylish and

classic…always in good taste;

You could wear that sensuous sundress;

Just right for Summertime, back out, shoulders

glistening as you sip your moscato underneath the

moonlight

Smile so radiant…you look at me…I look at you…yet

there is still another look I'd love to see on

you…something more meaningful and precious that

I'd love to do;

So stand beside me, and hold my hand

Gaze into my eyes with glee and surprise

Expectations

Heart-pounding palpitations

And I think…

I've seen you in every outfit

With style and finesse

But NOTHING in the world looks better to me

than you standing beside me in your wedding dress

Warm Rain

Warm rain
Tiny miracles
I feel them cascading,
falling upon my skin
Bringing forth emotions deep inside of me
that I've tried so, so hard to keep within,
Soothing to the core,
massaging each pore
Make it truly difficult
to ignore
As you take in...
each melody
And your kiss is telling me..
That I shouldn't stop
Fighting or ignoring,
This feeling that's come over me
The orchestra strings ring
Deep within my soul
Like a gentle crescendo
The warmth of the rain caresses our bodies as I'm
wrapped up in your caress,
The rain oozing through our clothes,

providing an exquisite layer of tenderness,
emancipating my every emotion with every touch…
It's just too much to simply take in, hold or clutch
And as the sun goes down,
The smoldering orange sun
fading into the dusky blue,
Eventually changing into the darkest hue of
midnight blue,
I want more of you…
I want ALL of you…
For my soul
is so openly exposed,
And your kiss is drenched in passion,
Having blown my mind
In the most seductive fashion,
I have everything to lose,
And the whole world to gain,
I think all of these things,
As I kiss you sweetly and seductively…
as we stand so closely
In the warm rain

Dipped

You're the strawberry dipped in chocolate
Rich and creamy like a tasty fondue
A simple bite of your fruit covered in cocoa
reminds me of how sweetly you rendered your due
Immerse me in your love, cover me, enrich me, love
me, seduce me, honor me, complete me;
I can't believe that you love me so much,
Tender to the touch,
you are just too much
I've never felt sensuality
Your lips are succulent, delectable, tasty, kissable
When you speak to me,
your words are winsome, seductive, encouraging,
irresistible
I can't believe how sweet you are;
Girl, you are so well-equipped
You're the strawberry dipped inside my chocolate...
I'm so into you...
Baby...I'm dipped...

Sip Tea With Me

Sip tea with me
Take in the moment
Ever so gently and slowly
Savoring every taste, every smile, every glance
As my taste buds salsa and tango
Evolving into the sweetest dance
Sip tea with me
Let's relax and chill
Shall it be African nectar or Chamomile?
The choice is yours
As my deep emotions cascade through to your open
doors
You take me in the way that your lips
take in Earl Grey or Moroccan Mint
Enamored with the very thought of you
It's as if you are heaven sent
Sip tea with me
I promise to make it worth your while
Allow me to ginger you with my charm,
masculinity, and style,
I'll listen intently and be sweet to you like
honey in your tea
If only you would sip tea with me

My Lips

My lips
girl don't look at my lips...
The ones that you say are well-defined...
looking at them may get you in trouble,
yes... the good kind
The kind in which our bodies are interwoven and
intertwined
Who knows how deep we would love?
or how much joy and satisfaction we would find?
What I do know is that when your workday is
long...
my strokes will be longer...
and when your desire to be with me is strong,
You will know that I feel the same way too...
But only stronger...
You say that into my
eyes you must not stare
For if you gaze too long
I might just take you there
Take you to the place
Where you would be locked up
In a jail filled with passion and ecstasy
Your love to me would come so easily

That it would be considered a first-class felony
My tenderness would be relentless
As I love you with guile and finesse
within the bounds of my strong, yet gentle caress
But I wouldn't use my lips just for the pleasure I
would place upon your skin
I'd use my lips to delicately lace your heart and
soul with beautiful words that come from deep
down within
I'd encourage you and make sure that
you are built up spiritually
while everyday making sure to let you that I love
you
For you are my every fantasy and innermost reality
So although I'm not able to partake of
your treasures
just yet
My lips are waiting...
To place upon your lips
A kiss that you will NEVER forget

Enchantress

Enchantress
My beautiful dark chocolate temptation
You're taking me on this journey of love
A one-way ticket,
A never-ending, paradisaic destination
I want to take this ride with you,
Me with the crazy laugh, cappuccino-colored eyes,
romantic ways and the heart of a gentleman,
You with the deepest sincerity, trueness of friendship,
supple lips, a sundress and a sexy pedicure
The trip of a lifetime, a voyage
Filled with love and romance
Slightly innocent, but real and pure;
My bags are packed, my conscience is clean and steady,
I'm hearing you whisper to me, "Baby…I'm ready…"

Enchantress
My beautiful dark chocolate temptation
Your spirituality keeps me lifted
Your sensibility keeps me sane

The thought of your sweetness
Constantly stays with me
Never allowing my heart and soul to ever
wander or wane;
With you, I never need to wonder, hope or imagine
how good love will be
Just understand: the mere thought of you
will keep me in ecstasy
Your dark chocolate kisses will be so alluring
Forever in my heart and mind they will be
enduring,
everlasting, pervading through my soul
for the longest of time
So gentle on my skin…so, so, divine

Enchantress
My beautiful dark chocolate temptation
You hold me with your charm
You truly fascinate me
Your gentle compassion, warm friendship, your
sense of humor
are all so wonderful to me,
they allow me to be liberated, to be exquisitely free,
to be the spiritual, loving, romantic man I am
the man of Jehovah I need to be

So Enchantress
My beautiful dark chocolate temptation,
Continue to love me and care for me
Until our next meeting, our next conversation
Our next glance...
Just know that I love you
And look forward to the time
When we can share that morning cup of coffee...
and that eternal slow dance

One Stare, One Glance

One stare, one glance
One touch, one dance
One kiss, one chance
One love, one romance

One day in the Fall
with Autumn leaves falling
from the sky,
I would listen
as the trees would sway and dance while the
westward breezes,
so warm and refreshing,
would softly sigh and cry...
the moment put me in a trance
A delightful melody,
with a sensual undertone
resonating deep within my soul
through my flesh,
to my marrow,
within my loins
Down to the bone
Unforgettable sensitivity
An unrelenting flow

A thoughtful whisper
Baby, how did you know?
That I loved you all of this time
For all of these years?
Did my seductive gaze give it away?
Was there something you needed to know,
something I needed to say?
You knew it all, felt it all...
The way I gazed at you...
said it all

One stare, one glance
One touch, one dance
One kiss, one chance
One love, one romance

Caress at Midnight

Love so deep,
No mere infatuation
It's a perfect scenario
The sweetest situation
My heart burns for your love
It's love's desperation
Let me get you in the mood
We'll slip into our love mode
My love is reserved just for you
It's you I have to hold
My heart yearns to tell you
Of pleasures untold

When it comes to sharing love
Our love gets deeper by the touch
As time flows on and on
We miss each other much too much
But nothing will be missed tonight
For your beauty will indeed be a sight
Our love will scale the greatest height
When I caress you at midnight

Kisses full of passion
They almost feel unreal
Your every touch
Tells of the ecstasy I feel

My love for you
No more I can't conceal
I love to whisper your name
Show you how good love feels
I'll caress you through the morning dawn
If that is what your heart wills

When it comes to sharing love
Our love gets deeper by the touch
And as time flows on and on
We miss each other much too much
But tonight I'll caress you
Our love will never be less
We'll caress each other at midnight
Enjoying our love finesse

After Love Expression

I'm your husband
You're my wife
We share some special things
So special in our life
With your love
I'm so enchanted
Never will I take your love for granted
And after love is made
You're basking in your sensuous glow
I'll you that I loved the way you loved me
These emotions I'll always show

After our love expression…
There's so much to say
Baby, I'll reveal everything
Skin on skin
Naked as we lay
This type of love that we share
I pray will never fade away
Such sweet discretion
Always leaves on my heart
An indelible impression
When it comes to our love expression

So let me caress your ankles
Kiss your fingertips
I feel your intoxicating ecstasy

When I kiss your lips
Baby, would you stay here beside me?
Please lie with me and talk for awhile
I'll smoothly place my hand inside of your hand
While you enamor me with your winsome smile
With strength and gentleness
I'll embrace your waist
I'll need all of time in the world to love you
I'll take my time loving you
No rushing, no haste
As you innately stroke your finger
Gently across my face
Ooooohhh, you give me such beautiful love
Sweet, sweet love
Intimate, such feminine grace
This type of love that we share
I pray will never fade away
Such sweet discretion
Always leaves on my heart
An indelible impression
When it comes to our love expression

So Intimate

I taste your sweet strawberry lip gloss
From our delicate, breathless kiss
And still, evermore, I feel
an unforgettable tenderness
That I never want to miss
I've washed and massaged your feet
After walking in the sand
Please understand
That you give me such great pleasure
When you touch and caress my hand
I'll rub the spots that need gentle care
It's intimate and I vow on my life to take you there
So take me in your arms
Just hold me and never let me go
Baby, you're the only one
That can please me
How much I love you
I'll always show
Let's not miss this moment
Timeless
So close to you
Forever and ever

Just as a luminant crescent moon
Hangs in the midnight, velvet of the Milky Way
Your sweetness and your kisses hang on the
strings that descend from the delicate silhouettes
from the back of my mind
You leave me speechless
With not a single word to say

Dark shadows through windows
An early morning glow
With you I'll share my love
All of me you will know
And after we make love
There's breakfast in bed
And as we sip Jamaican Rum cappuccino
I can't forget the sweet things that you said
Rose petals on my pillow
Your tenderness does show
You give me love I'll always need
Although I never told you so
So once again, I'll take my time
Sweetly loving you
Gently telling you
That all of my dreams have come true
Touching and teasing

Wooing and pleasing
This rendezvous I never want to forget
Your skin
Radiant and moonlit
I'm so close to you
Unbelievable
Your love is so Intimate

Cinnamon

A shade, a spice,
A scent so nice
Sweet enough on me to entice
Cinnamon
Baby, cool as ice
I had to think twice
You make me wonder
I ponder
On your pure perfection
A delightful collection of charm and affection
Cinnamon
The sweetest confection
Our kiss is a wish
From an afternoon daydream
Private times
An exotic scene alone
You know what I mean?
The love is shown
Check out the scene:
Grapes and cheese to please
A bubble bath and wine
With you
So sexy and fine

Enduring, alluring
A turquoise blue
Quality time spent
Just with you
Your kisses soothe me
You move me
In your arms is where I want to be
Marital bliss
Yes, you and me
A diamond on your ring finger
Causes a thought to linger
Sharing love in a special way
Exchanging vows on our wedding day
I waited for you and we took
The right way
My love for you will never sway…
My love for you
Is still special today
I wouldn't have it no other way

Cinnamon (Sweeter, Softer, and Deeper...)

Caress and squeeze me
You never tease me
Hearing your voice
Your tender whisper frees me
And I can't believe that loving you
Is so easy
Such ecstasy when you're here with me
Holding you in my arms
Your gentle skin
Gentle kisses from deep down within
But my love, it's not a sin
'Cause it's real love that you're living in
Wedding bells have rang
And you're my wife
You help me to deal with the stress and strife
That comes from working hard,
Dealing with the world
To provide us a good life
Coming home to you
I can really unwind
For you give me sweetness
A real peace of mind

A love like yours is so hard to find
Inner beauty, a spiritual mind
Yes, you're cinnamon
The special kind

Love Dance

Let me love dance with you
It's not that hard at all
I'll put hand around your waist
Deep in love we'll fall
I'll gently take your hands
Start to dream in your eyes
With grace we'll move across the floor
Whisper love lines to your surprise
We're caught up in our sensual groove
Accenting the way that we sway
Winelight shows an intimate move
As we love dance the night away
Exotic rhythms, smooth melodies
The sweetest sounding emotion
Let this dance symbolize our love
Unconditional, heart-felt devotion
You know that this is our favorite song
Sweet notes created for you and me

For this moment, I'll always long
To love dance eternally
Darling, let's make this time our own
To love dance is what I live for
Dim the lights, turn off the phone
We'll express our love forever more

Reveal Your Love To Me

Reveal to me
Passion and ecstasy
That's all within your mind
Baby, allow me
Let your precious heart see
True love you will find
I want to love you
As I love myself
My love knows no expense
Let me give you love
Darling, be good to yourself
And your heart won't suffer recompense

Feel the sweetness of my touch
Make you realize
I'm the love
For which your heart cries
I want to love you
As I love myself

Baby, be patient
Just you wait and see
You'll never know
Just how good love can be
Until you reveal your love to me

Baby, be patient
Just you wait and see
You'll never know
Just how good love can be

Afterthought Of Your Kiss

In a reflective mood
About you I'm reminiscing
Thinking of your love
And your kiss that I'm missing
Your kiss carries forth a passion
And a sweetness all it's own
Once my lips touch yours
All of my emotions are unleashed
Emotional and full-blown
I can't explain what comes over me
When I'm lost in your charms
Lost in the breath of your sweet kiss
When we're wrapped in each other's arms
It's such a small thing that we do
But it means so much
You'll never comprehend the love I feel
When our lips gently touch
But it's just an afterthought
An afterthought of your kiss

Our love could be so intimate
Now is never too soon
I'd love you to a state of bliss

Sheer seduction beneath a silver moon
It would start with your tender kiss
So vital to our romance
I'd love and adore you forever
All we need is just once chance
But it seems to be a mere afterthought
Something hoped for, never seen
Like in a romantic fantasy
Or a sweet afternoon daydream
Your kiss tickles my soul
Delicately teasing and playing with me
As I left with passion to give
For the deep love that may never be...
But it's just an afterthought
An afterthought of your kiss

Unspoken Romance

So unusual
I've experienced this before
Love without words
I'm left wanting more and more
You romance my mind
Although nothing is said
As my yearning for true romance
By you is fed

I won't say a word,
I'll let the moment speak for itself
As I'll lose my mind amongst
Your beauty, charms, and spiritual wealth
Your eyes utter forth words
That do no less than thrill
As your unmistakable gaze
Makes my spine
Oooohhh, tingle and chill
Oh, we'll play a game
See how much about one another
We really know
For it's to you and only you
My love I'll truly show

So baby be quiet
I've got it all figured out
I know all of the ways in which
I will satisfy you and please you
Without a shadow of a doubt
I trust that you'll love me sweetly
For we know
what good love is all about
There's no need to discuss our love
I know every intimate thought,
Deepest secret
Every exotic fantasy
That you're thinking of

What's In Your Kiss?

We're talking love
So confidential
One on one
Our love potential
I feel that this love is not
A mistake
For real love, true love
Is not coincidental
Just intimate, romantic
And supremely sensual

To hold your hand
Was a sweet thing
So innocent
Your caress brought me closer
To your tantalizing, romantic scent
Then to kiss your lips
Was such a beautiful task
So surreal
It left my senses reeling
With many questions to ask

What's in your kiss, baby?
It says so much to me
What's in your touch, sugar?
Oooohhh, sweetness
How could it be?
Was it just a feeling
Or something that we missed?
What's in your kiss baby?

We kissed
Down raindrops came
So many questions to ponder
Will our friendship
Ever be the same?
We know that love
Is so serious
We know that love is not a game
Could our desire to give so much
Our romantic natures be the blame?

But my love…
Your tender kisses
So fulfilling, so alluring
My heart soars straight
To the heavens

It's your love I'm after
Your love I'm pursuing
For you to hold me tightly
Was soul soothing
Most reassuring
On and on
Your kisses linger
Forever they're enduring

What's in your kiss, baby?
It says so much to me
What's in your touch, sugar?
Oooohhh, sweetness
How could it be?
Was it just a feeling
Or something that we missed?
What's in your kiss baby?

Let's Not Fight Anymore

Honey, let's not fight anymore
Why are we angry?
What are we fussing for?
We both know that it is
Something small and minute
Honey, we can talk it over
And end this senseless dispute
For you know that I hate when
Your eyes cut and pierce right through me
We get uncomfortable and love is never
The way that it should be
Sometimes I don't know what to say
Or know what to do...
All I know is that I should be loving you
So please understand my point of view
And I'll understand how you feel
We can then come together as one again
And make love over and over again
So sweet and so real
I'll be slow to speak
Quick to listen
I love it when you smile at me
As your countenance begins to glow

And your skin starts to glisten
I'll never leave your warm caress
And you'll never walk out that door
The candles are lit
Your favorite coffee is waiting
Baby, let's just love one another
Kiss me now
Let's not fight anymore

ABOUT THE AUTHOR

Thomas Ricardo Baker(born on April 29, 1968) has been writing poetry and prose for over thirty years and has been an educator for nearly twenty-five years. Armed with a B.A. in English: Writing, from the University of Tennessee at Chattanooga(1991) as well as possessing a Master's Degree in Education from Lee University (2004), his experiences as an educator, poet and writer have allowed him to travel the globe to such places as Brazil and the United Arab Emirates. His work and performances have been well received from many over the years. His hobbies include cooking, writing, art, sports, coffee, and listening to jazz and R&B music.